WATERING THE DEAD

Winner of the 2006-2007 Transcontinental Poetry Award

Watering the Dead

Jason Irwin

Pavement Saw Press
Ohio

Editor & Layout: David Baratier
Duck Logo: Joe Napora
Cover Art: Hans Krusi

Blue Collar Review: "Lucky," "Pocket Knife & At The Grocery;" *Confrontation*: "Talk Of The Town;" *Living Forge*: "Some Days It's A Love Story & Cadillacs;" *Lumina*: "Main Street;" *Miller's Pond*: "Dingle, 1996;" *Pearl*: "Barcelona;" *Plainsongs*: "Driving, Iowa;" *Slipstream*: "Remembering Frankie Lugo;" *The Sycamore Review*: "Dog Days;" *The Same*: "Nowhere." Some of these poems also appeared in the chapbook *Some Days It's A Love Story*, by Slipstream Press, 2005.

The author would like to thank Gerry Crinnin, Kevin Pilkington, Sarah Lawrence College, The Chautauqua Writers Center, The Arts Council of Chautauqua County, Slipstream Press, The Buffalo News Poetry Page & his family and friends.

PAVEMENT SAW PRESS
321 EMPIRE STREET
MONTPELIER OH 43543
http://pavementsaw.org

Full length books are available through the publisher or through:
SPD / 1341 Seventh St / Berkeley, CA 94710 / 800.869.7553
Literary journals and chapbooks are only available through the publisher

Winner of the 2006-2007 Transcontinental Poetry Award
for an outstanding first-book collection of poetry or prose. We read yearly
from June 1st until August 15th. Send SASE for more information.

Pavement Saw Press is a not for profit organization, any donations are
greatly appreciated and are considerered as charitable tax donations under
section 501 (c) of the federal tax code.

CONTENTS

III Going Home

for Wendi Lee

Sing of the ordinary oak, the branch cut off by the ax, and the flower no one looks at.

—Antonio Machado

I. Watching My Mother Sleep

Nothing I Thought I Knew

Monday I was the last seat
in the back row, in Mrs. Miller's
fourth grade—next to Joe Larivy,
who picked his nose through Spelling
and *The Gettysburg Address*—dreaming
I'd be a policeman, secret agent
or quarterback for the Buffalo Bills one day.

Tuesday I woke to the radio.
The announcer talked about a man
I'd never heard of, shot
the night before.
All day the TV, radio and newspapers spoke
his name. They said he was a singer.
My mother said it reminded her
of when Bobby Kennedy was killed.
It was the first time I'd seen her cry
since my father moved out.

Sunday, a memorial service interrupted
grandpa's football. My cousin and I
sat in front of that giant, oak-trimmed Zenith,
watched thousands crying in the rain
outside Lincoln's Memorial.
They played one of his songs, the lyrics spun
in my brain like a scratched record:
I am the Walrus, Goo goo goojoob, spun
like Monsignor Mengie's Good Friday sermon,
and in that moment I knew
nothing I thought I knew before mattered,
that somehow I was saved.

Main Street

From the front porch we guessed
colors of cars, drank lemonade
out of paper cups and listened
to the Kapinski kids get beat
by their mother. That dissonance
reverberated through back yards
where Virgin Marys kept vigil
in bathtub grottoes, and old man Tilly,
senile and drunk, promised
to pulverize us for throwing rocks
at his truck. Twenty years now

since he surrendered
to the Elks Memorial Home and the Kapinskis
moved to some God forsaken
Des Moines, or South Dayton,
after their mother's fourth husband
realized he was a woman, trapped
in the wrong movie, I think of them,
wonder what became of Priscilla,
who showed me her privates
behind the rabbit cage when we were nine,
or Timmy and George, who were all teeth,
sandy hair and bruises
no one ever questioned, not even
Miss Butler, who taught third grade.

I remember Sally, too,
blue as the swimming pool where they found her,
too young to cross the street alone
or read *Hamlet*. Sometimes I drive
by the old house on Main Street,
I can still see them:
faces and fists against glass.

Dog Days

That was the summer my father
took an axe to our picnic table
and my mother began
a ten year affair with Jesus.
The Ayatollah Khomeini replaced
Darth Vader
as the number one bad guy in the universe.
I was nine years old and still a dog,
barking through the house
in my fuzzy feet, with no idea
where Tehran was, or what divorce meant.

ZAVARELLA AND THE MATADOR

At Zavarella's barber shop we sat
on black vinyl chairs; my mother
picked through a half dozen magazines
and I, entranced by the velvet matador
that hung on the wall, and the framed photos
of Dean Martin, Rocky
Marciano, the Pope, that red head
in a bikini licking her lips.

Amid the strange fraternity of old men,
who gathered, with Brylcreem in their hair,
moles growing out their ears
and years of reluctantcy under the belts
they fastened too high above their waists,
I lost myself, inhaling the carnival-like fragrances
of talcum powder, aftershave, Lysol and cigars,
watching them admire their reflections in the mirror
and listening to their talk of sports,
politics, the weather and work.

Their groaning voices like kettle drums
and sick bassoons, played off each other
in perfect counterpoint as Sam Zavarella—
tattoos and pompadour—worked his magic,
clipping a bit here, a bit there, scissors
chirping like birds in his thick hands
and each lock of hair that fell
to the floor was an epiphany.

All Saint's Day, 1987

It was a Sunday,
the day after Halloween.
I was walking to church, hung
over, from drinking
Genny Cream Ale
out of mayonnaise jars
in Scott Jagoda's garage.
In my pockets,
a bunch of *Three Musketeer* bars,
Joe Rancka stole
From a kid dressed as Superman
on Deer Street.

My feet slid on the icy sidewalk
as a man came out
his front door, walked up
to me and asked if I knew
his daughter, Pam Cushing.
Yes, I said, all the while
looking at his eyes
that didn't appear
to be looking at anything.

She was killed last night,
he said, as calm
as if he were telling me
what he ate for breakfast.
You know Ryan Hayes?
He was driving, tried to beat
a train on Roberts Road.
Everyone died. Six of 'em,
he concluded in the same
monotone and walked back
into his house.

I stood watching the screen door
slam against its frame, trying
to understand what
had happened, then continued
on my way, thinking
there probably wouldn't be
school on Monday.

SUNDAYS

for Aiesha

And then there were those Sundays,
sitting in the uncut
dandelion grass at grandma's, our minds
racing with plans we'd soon forget,
our stomachs aching
from too much cola and lemon
meringue. You'd always cry
when it was time to go home,
you with that space
between your front teeth,
toilet paper tied in tiny bows
in your hair, and me
with my suspenders and plaid pants,
whispering naughty words
to make you laugh,
holding a magnifying glass between the sun
and a caterpillar, wondering did God
do the same to us.

First Communion

Dressed in a suit from JC Penney's
the color
of my grandfather's Pontiac,
all eyes were on me.
I made my way, slow
down the center aisle.
In front of me, Dean Valentine,
in his brother's pin stripes
and above us, on the wall to the left,
Jesus, hanging from his cross.
Even though it was a creamy plaster
I could still see the blood dripping down,
like the magic maker drawings I made
in Mrs. Kirst's art class.
Standing before Monsignor Mengie
I closed my eyes, opened my mouth
and received the body of Christ.
I knew it was only a matter of time
before I walked on water, healed the sick,
died the hero's death.

BURGETT'S REGENT

Years before movie-plexes and Blockbusters,
Joe Rancka, Mike Pakulski and I
would go to that chapel-like hall
of velvet and brick—owned by old Burgett
and his basset hound—on the corner
of Third and Washington,
with its leaky roof and stench of vomit,
perfume and sex; which at the time
we only knew about from the lectures
Dean Valentine's cousin, Art Maloney—
who got kicked out
of St. Elizabeth's for punching a nun—
gave us on our way home from school.

There in the front row, with our communion
of buttered popcorn, Ju Ju Bees and Milk Duds
we watched that white wall explode
into color, transforming us into those gods
we worshipped, with unquestioning faith:
Luke Skywalker, Rocky Balboa, Indiana
Jones, some Sho-Gun Warrior
and we forgot—for a couple of hours at least—
math class, Thursday Mass, the treat
of nuclear war and all those other traumas
that made up our daily lives.

April, 1989

Grandpa whistled through grandma's cancer seizures
and called on Christ's whiskers
to help the Yankees come from behind
to beat *those* Indians.

Easter came and went, without eggs
or candy that year.
I learned to drive and counted the days
till high school was over.
Some days I hung out with friends, or drove
my mother's car till the gas was gone.

Other days, I sat on the living room floor,
watched my mom and aunt Stephanie wipe drool
from grandma's chin,
after the shaking and rattling
of bed rails stopped.
They patted her forehead with a damp
cloth, fluffed her pillow and stroked
her hands, hands too weak
to stir spaghetti sauce, or grasp
Rosary beads. Grandpa just stared
straight ahead, cursing the TV.
Between innings he locked himself in the bathroom.
I pretended I didn't hear him sob
over the running water.

Puerto Rican Rum

Saturday nights when we were fourteen,
Joe Rancka and I sat in his room,
amid basketball trophies and *Playboys*,
getting drunk off a liter of Puerto Rican Rum,
listening to music, talking about how good
Jenny Elstrom looked, newly sprouted,
poking through a white T-shirt after gym.
Saturday nights while his parents were out
at the clubs, we sat there getting stupid
ass drunk, the way small town kids get drunk,
with nothing to do, but get kicked out
of movies, or go to keg parties that always
got busted by the cops.
We talked about leaving this town one day
and never coming back, vowed
we'd never smoke dope, until one night
after confirmation class,
when Jimmy Syminski bought a bag of weed
and we smoked it in Joe's garage.
We vowed we'd be friends forever,
then, the summer after high school,
when I was preparing for community college,
he got caught burglarizing houses
he used to deliver newspapers to and spent
ten years in and out of prisons
all over the state. Now
I go to the bars after my shift
at the grocery store, sometimes
I run into Joe. We have a few beers,
talk about his game winning shot
in eighth grade, all the friends
we haven't seen in years,
like Jimmy Syminski and Jenny Elstrom,
think about all the girls we never screwed
and those Saturday nights when we were fourteen,
drinking Puerto Rican Rum.

ODE

for Todd Dopler: 1968-2000

It had been six months since we saw each other,
the morning I heard you died—
Mother's Day,
a high speed chase, a stolen car.
I went to the store, bought a six pack
and drove around till I was buzzed
enough to cry.

I remembered that day you pissed
in the dressing room trash can
at JC Penney's,
our crazy road trips to Bear Lake,
Jamestown and New York
City, all those late night calls
from pay phones and jail.

I know if I were truly a good friend,
I wouldn't have walked out
on you that night
at *The Village Limits*,
I would've turned back, when you called.

At the funeral home you lay in the casket
in a suit and tie, head turned
so no one could see
half your face gone, eyes
sewn shut.
You looked so peaceful
I wanted to tell you
to quit fucking around.

I could hear you calling me,
accusing me,
like it was my fault.
I felt like I was being suffocated,
like I was being pulled
into a void
I only half lusted for,
so I ran, but this time
you followed.

For weeks and weeks I felt you near me,
following me.
I felt your eyes watching me.
Nights I drove around town
with you,
there in the front seat, trying
to drive you away again.

SUMMER IN SUSSEX

The summer I turned sixteen
I spent at my cousins' in Sussex,
New Jersey. Each morning I'd sit
at the kitchen table listening
to the stories my uncle Nef told
and retold: how in 1932
he organized the city's first
mens' softball league, the year
the Columbus Club won
the Monday night bowling championship,
about the deli he ran
for fifty odd years and the trips he took
with his wife—my grandmother's older sister,
Rose—to Yankee Stadium,
Niagara Falls and Youngstown, Ohio.
I remember staring at his black shoes
when he shuffled from one chair
to another, unable to find comfort,
or the way light sometimes reflected
off the pens he kept in his breast pocket.

Afternoons he'd snore through his favorite
soap operas—his salt-swollen ankles
oozing through socks—
waking to the smell and sizzle of dinner
grilling on the deck. He'd eat his fill
only to demand, *When are we going to eat?*

Nights I'd lie in bed listening to him
down the hall, screaming for his mother
and I'd think of that girl—
whose name I didn't know, whose face
I'd never seen—in the room next to mine
at the hospital when I was ten,
who screamed all night for the nurse.
I didn't cry for the girl
or my uncle, but maybe out of guilt
for ignoring them both, maybe

out of fear that one day it would be me,
alone in a room, crying
for a life too quickly lived,
for comfort that could not be found.

Watching My Mother Sleep

I come home from work to find my mother
asleep on the couch, clutching
a pillow, curled
like a child, a coffee cup, pack
of *Old Gold Filter 100s*, a lighter
and the ashtray I made
in fourth grade
on a stool beside her.

I stand there and trace the lines
in her face with my eyes, slow
my breathing to match hers
and think of all the times
I've watched her sleep.

Those school day mornings
when her alarm blasted
me awake and I'd hurry
to the kitchen, turn on
the *Mr. Coffee* and make
toast, while she pressed snooze,
nights I'd lie in bed burning
with anticipation for her
good night kiss,
to feel her lips press mine:
all those nights
when I was in the hospital,
I'd stare at her as she slept in a hard,
upright chair.
I remember nights her screaming
woke me and I'd pull
the covers over my head, thinking
it would make her nightmares stop.

Watching her now I wonder
if she still dreams
the dreams of childhood:
of ballerinas and tea parties,
wildflowers, dreams
of the dead.

I wonder if she's ever
really been happy,
if she cries

when no one is around,
if she thinks I've been a good son.

II. Lunch

BARCELONA

They were among the first settlers here,
not long after the war
for independence was won:
my father's people: square jawed,
Scotch-Irish Presbyterian stock,
fishermen, farmers and factory workers, all.
Pale as salt and stern as the God
that sent down fire
on Sodom and Gomorrah.
These are the people I never knew,
but know, through photos, yellowed
by so many seasons, my grandmother left
when God, in his mercy, blessed her
one October day with a stroke
and she was free of widowhood,
colon cancer and cataracts.
It was here, in Barcelona, New York,
on the southern shores of Lake Erie,
that once swelled with whitefish, blue pike
and herring, where the first
gas powered lighthouse was built
in 1829—where my father was born—
here, where Dr. Thomas Branwell Welch
invented a way to preserve unfermented grapes,
where Grace Bedell: age eleven,
suggested to Abe Lincoln
that he "would look a lot better" if he grew
whiskers, here where the winters last
until mid summer, and here, where my life
will surely end, just as it began: a speck of dust,
lost in a universe that rarely acknowledges
the dreams of an ordinary man.

AT THE GROCERY

Between produce and discounted bread
a man shoves oranges
into his pockets. I want to tell him
take some apples, too,
a banana, avocado, a six pack, anything
that will help him through another day,
tell all the hungry to come and feast,
to feed them like Jesus
fed them in the Gospels. Instead
I walk to the deli, past Betsy,
up to her elbows in potato salad, famous
for her Christmas party striptease.

In the break room Tommy sits—
mop at his side, legs crossed, boot atop
steel-toed boot, going bald, alcoholic—
thumbing through a newspaper
he can't read.

What's up? he asks, as I sit down,
eye the clock: quarter of four,
fifteen minutes before I punch out and he
punches in. *Not much,* I reply, notice
a pallet of canned foods waiting
to be stocked and think how I've worked
at this store for one year
and six months. Too long, and I think
how my father and grandfather worked,
of all the dreams they must've swallowed
to put food on the table, pay the mortgage
and know I'm not that faithful or strong.

POCKET KNIFE

Sitting on the back porch steps
by the raspberries' rebellion,
I finger your tobacco stained
Kingston pocket knife
as if it were a magic lamp
that might connect me
to you, once more.

The knife you chipped
Captain Black from your pipe
with; hands, fingers swollen
from Gout and Arthritis, hands
that shoveled coal
into steel plant furnaces
for forty years, taught me
to peel an apple, hold a bat.

The same knife you gave me
for my tenth birthday I swore
I lost playing kickball.
The same knife Uncle Joe found
in a kitchen drawer, looking for money
and old baseball cards,
above where grandma kept
aprons, buried in a mass grave
of empty Scotch tape
dispensers, matchbooks
and expired coupons.

Found, the day after your funeral,
like that photograph
in an old cigar box
on the cellar stairs: you
in Wallace, Idaho,
summer, 1933
stranding so proud
on that rocky bluff, hands
deep in denim pockets,
dimpled smile, thick
Dago hair,

looking like I look now:
age thirty,
wishing I had the courage
to hug you more.

DINGLE, 1996

On the dirt road that winds to Dunquin—
Ireland's most western point—
I stand on the edge
of a cliff, look out toward Slea Head
and the Blasket Islands.
It's October, I'm twenty-five,
on my own for the first time.

I can still taste stout on my lips,
still hear the echo
of uilleann pipes from a pub
in town, where I stood among locals
and stared at an old fisherman,
trying to imagine what his life had been like
on the high seas, the heartache
he hid behind his white beard, the patch
that covered his left eye,
or the scar that ran down his face.

Standing on that cliff—
visions of Stephen Dedalus,
wayward in *Nighttown*,
stagger in my brain—
I think of my father's ancestors
who sailed from these shores
nearly three hundred years ago
and wonder what it would be like never
to go home again, to lie down
in the tall grass,
to breathe the salty air,
to be able to once again
look at my hands with astonishment,
to see them as the fantastic sea creatures
they once were; to become God,
or simply a spire of smoke.

TUESDAY NIGHT SIGN-IN

Tuesday nights it's Dom Polski's
with Mike, who I've known
since we fought over who
was the *real* Batman
at our kindergarten Halloween party.

Inside, amid the thick swelter
of cigarette smoke and cheap beer,
the banter of everyday:
work, football, taxes, the weekend,
a drone nearly drowning
the music pulsing from the jukebox.

We claim two stools
next to a statue of Saint Stanislaus,
who guards a roll of raffle tickets
and *Lion's Club* mints
and order a couple of drafts from Cecil,
he's tended bar here longer
than anyone can remember.

Mike tells me about his son, Ryan,
who's learning to walk and talk;
he tells me about all the arrests
he's made this week: the drunk
and disorderly, domestics, crack
addicts and petty thieves.

I never used to hate people, he smiles, *until
I became a cop.* Our conversation turns
to our friend Joe Rancka, who
was a star basketball player
at St. Elizabeth's, in prison now, six years
after the burglaries. Pondering Joe's fate
I notice a woman a few seats down.
She looks just like Tracy Sarzyniak, who died
of Leukemia at sixteen.

For a moment I'm stunned,
remembering how beautiful she was, maybe

too beautiful for this town, built
and abandoned by the railroad and steel
industry. I think of all the kids I've known
who have died, the ones hit by trains,
the ones who drove too fast, blew
their brains out or OD'd. I look around
at all the faces, people I've known
all my life and wonder
if I know them at all.

Someone announces Eugene Kapuchinski won
the jackpot. He buys a round
for everyone. In the uproar I turn to Mike,
we laugh, drink the clear liquid
and order another, forgetting
how much it will hurt in the morning.

REMEMBERING FRANKIE LUGO

How many nights I listened to your tears
in that dark bar with skeletons on the wall,
we mistook for heaven?
All those beers you lingered over
how I was the only kid in the neighborhood
who didn't hold it against you for being
Puerto Rican. Yet that wasn't half
as heroic as the beatings you endured
from your father: knuckles white,
clenching the chin-up bar as leather slapped
your shoulder blades, and your mother,
how I can still envision her, standing squat,
pointing a finger at you like a pistol
from the other side of the hedges.
She put an end to so many summer
baseball games against the Kapinski kids,
and you, the dutiful son, always
surrendered. How many hours she kept you
on your knees praying Jesus' forgiveness
I don't want to know.
I was too green even then, the day you proclaimed yourself
to my cousin Amanda, who was all
of seven years old with curly hair and scabby elbows.
And now I write you letters I'll never send,
too embarrassed by the passing years
to call your sister Miriam and ask
what prison you're in.
All I know is you're out there, somewhere in time,
like a myth or dream that somehow
finds its way back. All I know
are the stories that travel the way all bad news travels.
The one about your young bride, the little girls,
the dresses you bought and made them
try on, the Polaroids, the love
only you could understand.

TOKYO AND THE RIO GRANDE

I was not yet twenty-six that January
I drove cross country
with two women, one of whom
I was foolishly in love with—for she
was in love with a herbologist from LA—
and the other one, who chewed bubble gum and talked
about nothing but Brad Pitt and Scientology—
we picked up at a diner
outside Mobile, and though I'd been to Ireland
and Bermuda, it was my first time
west of Ohio.

On Interstate 40, somewhere between Bluewater
and Thoreau, my head buried
in the pages of a road atlas, my fingers
following our course, I marked off
cities and towns we passed
and remembered how, as a child
I'd sit for hours, gazing at maps, transfixed
by longitudes and latitudes, infatuated
by topographies, maps of rainfall
distribution, ocean currents,
vegetation and mineral maps,
maps that show the relative motion
of tectonic plates, changes
in sovereignty, military advances
and retreats. How I was smote
with historical maps, grew dizzy
over political and population maps,
maps that measured the depths of oceans,
lengths of rivers, world maps, regional maps and city maps.

All these maps filled me with a longing for some place
Other, like the stories my Uncle Joe told,
of his days in Buffalo, Boston and New York,
wandering streets, working in a garment factory, selling
his blood for wine and being rejected
by the Nation of Islam because he was white—
Each time I opened an atlas
those wondrous melodies and rhythms

played in my ears, places ten years
after that first cross-country trip

I still have yet to see:
Zanzibar, Marrakesh, Calabria
and Wolverhampton, Argentina,
Pakistan, Tokyo
and the Rio Grande.

LUCKY

Mornings I stand on the loading dock
with a cup of black coffee, smoke
two Kool Menthols and watch the sun
rise over the tin roofs
and water tower across the river.
There's a peacefulness in these moments
like I remember as a boy,
delivering newspapers up and down
Clinton and Washington Streets.

The stench of the dog food factory used to make me sick,
but after twenty-five years on line #7—
the same line my old man
had a heart attack on—
I've grown used to it, feel it's a part of me,
like the back aches and stiff joints,
like this town and all the disappointments a man gathers,
like lint or coins in his pockets.

My father bought me a lottery ticket
the day I started here and told me,
if I was lucky I'd better get the hell out.
A dog food factory was no place
for a man to grow old in.

I buy a ticket every day at Earl's
and every day think of Kenny Burns,
that night we got drunk in Hong Kong
and he promised me a gig on his uncle's shrimp boat
in Galveston when we were through with the Navy.
Hell yes! I hollered, but ended up
back here, married Elizabeth, rented
a two bedroom and started at three
twenty-five an hour on 2nd shift.

My oldest son , Tommy turned 18.
I took him out for breakfast at Millie's
Diner asked him what
he wanted to do with his life.
He says he wants me to get him a job

on the line. I buy him a lottery ticket
and say No!

Don't fuck up like I did.
This ain't no place to grow
old in, but he's stubborn like me.
He never listens to his father.

FOR MIKE, GOING TO WAR, AGAIN

Has it been that long, twenty years
since we patrolled the neighborhood—
Deer Street, Leopard, Main—
dressed in our thrift store camouflage,
toy machine guns at our side, canteens
full of *Kool-Aid*? You thirteen and I
twelve, the year I had the home tutor,
and we spent New Year's Eve
listening Billy Idol and *The Police,*
smoking candy cigarettes,
dreaming of war.

How about that letter we wrote Melvin Tilly,
informing him
he was under surveillance
by the Junior Green Berets?
We watched triumphantly
from the Kapinski's swing-set
Efran Lugo take the blame,
his mother decking him
right there in the driveway
with a powerful left..

Last night we talked on the phone
for the first time in years.
You are now a father,
years after
your own father died.
Remember his laugh,
the way he sang his love for Jesus
at those basement revivals
our mothers' dragged us to?
I can still see him
playing a broom like a guitar,
dancing Chuck Berry style.

Today I'm in New York,
writing poetry, checking email
and you, in Texas,

preparing to go to war
again, the second time
in twelve years. I pray
you courage and a safe return.

DRIVING, IOWA

Heat swirls like water in the distance,
pulling in grain towers and crows
in its imagined under-tow.
This unleavened landscape, an eternity of corn
and telephone poles.
Patches on the highway like Arabic
or Jackson Pollock.
Your beard— a house painter's
used up bristles— talks to me
in the rear-view mirror,
of the California dream
and the divinity of man,
as we cruise through Winterset:
birthplace of John Wayne,
praying for Omaha or rain.

Love Poem #125

You say it's all in the fingers
when I'm down there
rubbing your toes,
the way your blood clots
when the bath is boiling
and the sheets are cold,
how the rhythm of my intent
makes you quiver.

I like the way you taste
when you're cranky,
nights when the moon
plucks a B flat
and that gleam in your eyes
when you're about to bite.

HOLY THURSDAY
for Walt Poland: 1930-2004

Despite the rain I take a long walk,
in search of a quiet bar,
where old men brood
over fifty-cent drafts and talk of a past
more real than any future.

At noon I pass St. Elizabeth's
where Monsignor Mengie preaches
about those last hours in Gethsemane
and asks the congregation for a second collection.
Across the street, the movie theater
Barb Johnson taught me how to kiss
in, stands like a tomb.
Under the viaduct where the Amtrak
used to stop is flooded, smells of pigeon shit
and gasoline. Down Third Street
I cut through the lot where the pet shop
burned and enter *The Friendly Tavern*,
soaked and shivering. I take a seat
next to Walt, who's spitting Morse Code.
He looks like Lazarus:
caught somewhere between this world
and the next.

Where you been you little shit?
he says, his face of dry clay
cracks into a smile and his eyes,
blue as Heaven, look at me
with a strange tenderness. He wipes
his beard of foam and proceeds
to enlighten me on the price
of chopped ham, bananas
and chicken thighs at P & G
Grocery, He tells me
about the one armed fiddler,
who used to play here in the 30's,
about Korea and his first wife,
whom he married after the war.
I order a pitcher from Brenda—

the green butterfly she keeps
between her breasts
makes everyone sit up straight—
taking a sip of beer, I finger the Sacred Heart
key chain in my pocket, remember
giving it up for Lent
and switch to whiskey.

CADILLACS

Devout as priests, far enough
from their youth to bemoan
the changing times,
these working men—
sons of Sisyphus—toil
in the purgatory of
Monday through Friday, men
hard as gravel, shredded and torn,
fingers gone, stripped like old bolts.

Men like my father, who talked
about *Some Day,* as if
it were an actual date
like Christmas or the 4th of July.
Some day, he'd say,
when I save enough money
I'm gonna tell 'em
where they can shove it. Fuck 'em.
Thirty-five years for a watch
and hip surgery.

I see these men at night in diners
and bars, hunched and quiet, faces
cracked, bloodless, unused to sun
or smiles, read the papers,
playing numbers. Men broken
by the promises of a good, hard
day, promises made by men
without mortgages or used cars,
men with soft hands.

After last call they wander
the car dealers' with heavy feet
and lovesick eyes,
groping the Cadillacs
they will never buy.

TALK OF THE TOWN

Across the street Mr. Gambino collects
branches from his front lawn.
He looks like a potato picker
Van Gogh sketched,
forever bending.
A blue jay somewhere, unseen
nags him like his wife
who stands on the blacktop
pointing out sticks
and limbs he's missed.

In my kitchen the TV says
Jesus has been seen
wandering corn fields
in Nebraska, dressed
like a scarecrow, doing rain dances
for the locals.

Down the street Mrs. Anderson believes
her dead husband, Frank
is the Christ, boasting
of his nightly apparitions
to her Tuesday bridge club.

He never fucked this good
when he was alive, she confides
to Miss Walters, a fifty year old
math teacher, who blushes for her
innocence of love and men.

I pour another coffee, sit back
and think about that Mexican Madonna
at the bar last night
and how I'd give my right leg
to feel her breath
on my skin.

BETWEEN US

The third time you called
you screamed my name
and wanted to know why
I hadn't called you back.
You wanted to know how
I could just turn it off
like a light, just leave
the room with you
and everything in it.

I listened to your messages,
hung up the phone, flipped out
the light and walked
downtown to the park.

On a bench across from two lovers
I thought about those mornings
I used to sit in bed
watching flakes of sun
dance across your back and thigh
while you slept
and remembered how you used to say
I didn't need you
the way you needed me.
I thought about how long it had been
since nice words passed
between us and decided
not to call you back.

With My Father

Six o'clock in the evening, still
light out. My father and I
on a road trip together for
the very first time, a long
day on highways, at rest stops,
driving across New York State.
We check our things
at the Holiday Inn and set out
in search of a bar.
Three blocks away, a place
called *Mc Nabb's*. We sit
near the neon window. He
orders a *Labatt's Blue* and I a *Black
and Tan*. Smoke
from two guys with cigarettes
at the other end of the bar burns.
I don't complain, that's my father's job,
one of his few pleasures.

I watch our reflections in the mirror.
The thirty years that separate us seems
more like three hundred. On TV
men in suits discuss the war.
My father sips his beer and says
the only way to stop them
from fighting is to kill them all.
Blow 'em right off the map, then
there'll be peace.

I study the caverns that are slowly
swallowing his eyes,
eyes once green, have grown gray
and cloudy. I feel a mix
of sadness and anger swelling up;
thirty-two years worth of things
unsaid. Still I keep quiet,
maybe out of respect, maybe
out of fear of him, or for I might say
if I had the guts.

He tells me how hard
he works, while everyone else
stands around, shooting
the breeze, drinking coffee.
He tells me about all the things
he should've done, all
those years ago. I listen
attentively. I've heard
it all hundreds of times.
I listen like a priest
or psychiatrist, with no acts
of atonement or advice to give.

He tells me about all the things
he'd going to buy when he wins the Lottery:
a house in the *Keys*, maybe one
in Palm Springs like Sinatra, one
in Vegas, too. An SUV,
a sixty-four inch color TV, a blender
and a new mattress.
Maybe it's because I haven't spent
thirty-five years working in a factory,
but I get the feeling money won't
make him happy. I think
we are as different as two people can be.

Moments like these I search my mind
for something in common, something more
than blood. I think of those times
I rode atop his shoulders
through the woods
behind my grandmother's house.
Then, along a dirt path—the two of us
like a living totem pole—
he'd carry me to the beach,
where we'd look for driftwood
and sail boats on the horizon.
I remember the silence of those days,
the most beautiful silence we could find.

Lunch

At the city mission I sit down
next to Walt and Jimmy Young Bear—
a Cattaraugus Seneca—who goes
by James now, since he taught himself
to read at thirty-five.
Always quick with a dirty joke
and helping hand, today
he talks about layoffs
at the juice factory, cuts
in benefits, the pain in his back,
bills he's behind on
and his wife, Angela, who's pregnant again.
Nothing really changes, he says,
between spoonfuls of rice
and beans. *Look at all these faces*
they're the same faces I've seen here
for six years. It doesn't matter
who the president is, or the mayor,
or how good the TV says
the economy is doing. Fuck
the Dow Jones! All you gotta do
is look around.

I turn to Walt, whose beard is dripping
with coffee. *Mickey was too sick*
to come down, he says, *but Medicaid*
finally approved an electric wheelchair.
I look at the next table, at Art Murphy
and old King Leatherwood, at Scary Mary
and her six kids, and Max,
who used to be a math professor and agent
for the CIA until his mother died
and he went mad and buried her
in the trunk of his Buick.

After lunch I say goodbye to Walt and James.
I walk up Center Street in the cold
and snow and think about that verse in the Bible
where Jesus proclaims a rich man
will hardly ever enter
the kingdom of Heaven.

III. Going Home

WATERING THE DEAD

At the cemetery drive-thru
Jesus waves hello, blesses me
as I turn the radio off
and make the sign of the cross.

The headstones call out,
eager for a word or glance
from the living.
Their names take flight
in my mind: *Catalano,*
Vacanti, Bartalomaeu, Joe.

I walk to the sprinkler and remember
the old man who used to live
across the street: always
on his front steps, hands clasped, black
jacket, smiling. He'd throw
us the ball back, when one of us hit
a homerun. We called him Joe,
though my grandfather said
his name was Sal.

At my grandparents' grave I offer
a prayer, bend to pull weeds,
water the geraniums my mother planted
on Memorial Day.

Content among the dead, I sprawl
on the fresh cut grass, watch
an angel with a missing left hand,
arms outstretched, smiling
like Joe smiled.

I close my eyes and see him and my grandfather
sitting at a baseball game, or spaghetti
dinner. Some nights
they're the crickets outside my window,
singing me to sleep.

How We Hurt

The train rumbled past the same nameless
small towns I remembered, past
houses built of brick and wood, houses
with insulation showing like wounds,
past back yards where skinny dogs
stood tied to chains and cars,
on cinder blocks, looked like years
since they've seen blacktop.

Towns passed like a dream:
slow and hazy.
I wondered about the people
who lived in them, about their lives
and the hurt hiding behind those painted doors.

The winter sun reflected on white
frozen fields. It reminded me
of the bathtub in the house
where I grew up, how
it shined in the glow
of the light above the sink.

I thought of you, too,
the smell of lavender in your hair,
the way you moved
beneath me, and those nights
we lay entwined in a dark room,
promising each other things
we couldn't promise.

I thought of how we hurt
and all the little ways
we hurt each other,
again and again, trying
to protect ourselves
from some giant hurt,
from something
too painful to bare.

DIRT

for Eric

Look at the two of us, 80 degrees
and we're dressed like December,
sitting in a bar, drunk, at one in the afternoon,
comparing facial hair and socks,
talking about Henry Miller,
Brando and ex-wives.
You saying how nothing matters,
that we're nothing
but dirt and the only god
is this very moment.
Look at us, screaming into our pints,
telling stories like
that night in Buffalo, Brooklyn,
Jamestown or Fredonia:
the time we passed out
on the front lawn, me in a pile of leaves
and you, spread-eagled
with half a burrito in your mouth,
the night we stole candy bars
from the mini-mart and lost
the hubcaps to my car, driving for hours
on those county back roads,
that time outside Matt LaChusia's house
when three cop cars came speeding
down the street and the police frisked me
for knives while you were inside
taking a shit, or that night on 3rd Avenue,
we met that harpist from Long Island.
She was beautiful, looked like
Samuel Beckett and drank Bourbon
until we left without paying and woke up
on the A train at four in the morning in Flatbush
starving for corned beef hash.
Look at the two of us:
laughing at the lives
we should've lost years ago, all those nights
that blur into one.
Look at us: running from ourselves
with the belief that we may well be
nothing more than dirt.

Some Days It's A Love Story

At P & G Grocery the dairy manager
has a Bachelor's in Economics
and a pulled groin
from lifting crates of milk.
He's been writing the first chapter to a novel
for six years.
Some days it's a love story,
some days a comedy,
about people in a small town,
like the guy in aisle eight who fits
all he learned from his father
into his right hand and smacks his son
for asking too many questions,
or the cashier at express
who flirts with the younger bank teller
who comes in every day for lunch,
handing him change she smiles,
avoids his eyes and remembers
it's been over two years
since she's been kissed.
Outside, a factory worker, fresh
off the midnight trick
climbs into a beat up *Chevy*,
opens a can of *Milwaukee's Best*
he bought for breakfast, takes a sip,
sets it between his legs, keys the ignition
and thinks about the day his wife left,
complaining *he* was the one
who changed.

MORNING WITH CALEB

St. Georges, Bermuda

We sit on the balcony, my little cousin and I—
cereal bowls and apple juice at our side—
happy as two dogs, watching ships sail
on a lizard green sea.
Birds chirp in a nearby cedar.
Down the street a woman beats
her laundry.
I marvel at my cousin: three years old
and wide eyed, his hair a bramble
of black curls.
He laughs as he shoves a wad
of raspberry bubble gum in his mouth,
then revs a toy truck over my foot and asks why?
Why is the sky blue?
Why can't you stay here forever?
Why? Why don't the stars shine in the daytime?
I look at him and wonder
how can I explain that one day
he will forget this moment, that he'll grow
and become a man, fall
in love with a woman someday,
who is destined to break his heart,
that I will no longer be his best friend.
How can I explain
that the sky only looks blue,
that nothing in this life is forever, not
the quiet mornings after breakfast,
watching ships on the horizon,
nor the flavor of bubble gum,
that even in the brightest sun
night is lurking?

GET OUT

for Ed

The first light of morning fills the spaces
between tree branches and houses
along the avenue.
You scrape frost from the windshield
of a rented truck, blow
into your numb hands and watch
your breath escape, the way you plan to escape—
the way your father did
all those summertimes ago—
just get the hell out
with nothing to guide you,
save an overwhelming desire
you find hard to describe, that
uncertainty that grows down deep in men,
makes them question
the simple comforts and securities they've been taught
to be thankful for.
One thing you do know:
you won't grow old and die
in this town, with that desire still burning
your lips, when they lower you in the ground.
You won't work your life away
without taking that "talked about" chance.
Inside the truck you crank the radio,
light your last cigarette, inhale
and head south.
On the highway it all seems perfect,
the future spread out before you
like the most beautiful woman in the world.

They've Sold Your House

What more can I do
but talk to you
in those quiet moments
before sleep and dreams?

What more can I do
but make your memory a psalm
and offer my penance
for those times
I let the futility of days
get in the way?

They've sold your house
and someone else will be there
between the walls,
at the kitchen table
when morning's light
touches the counter top,
someone else in front of the TV,
someone else's laughter
through the walnut trees.

They've sold your house,
grandpa, and I will no longer
be able to visit, to stand
in that churchly emptiness of cold
and cobweb and curtains drawn,
straining for the smell
of tobacco and oranges,
no longer
the echo of your voice
and those familiar benedictions
of wooden nickels and provolone.

The Way A Storm Strikes

Late afternoon, I have sat on the front lawn
for hours, watching a regiment of ants
swirl around a small hole
in the ground and the long shadow
of an oak tree slowly cover me.
Its leaves are falling, gathering in piles,
then scattering with the wind,
and I can't help but wonder
if it's like that with us:
have we learned to die
that easily, more easily perhaps,
than we've learned how to live?
Do we just fall
from the safety of our own branch,
only to be forgotten?
Do we die so easily that sometimes
we don't even notice it
the way lights dim
in a movie theater,
the way a storm can sometimes strike:
without warning or apology?

Morning

I smile at the waitress filling my cup,
notice her earrings—little green cats—
the gold cross hanging
from her neck, the black and blue
under her right eye.
She smiles back and I follow her reflection
in the mirror. She walks behind me
to a table where a group of workmen
sit—rough chins atop scabbed
knuckles. One of them calls her Lucy,
another honey. Outside
the sun has barely climbed
above the rooftops, the city
is still in silhouette. A tall pine looms
amid leafless elm and maple trees
in the park across the street.
The waitress walks by me again, stops
in front of the mirror, fixes
her long brown hair, touches her bruise.
I watch and think, how easily I could love
her, on this beautiful, November morning:
the kind of morning I imagine
even Beethoven would enjoy
with a cup of black coffee
and no need at all for words.

Spared

I trembled when the nurse
placed a stethoscope on my chest,
felt my body burn
with a desire I couldn't explain.
I watched her check my temperature, blood
pressure and i.v. then close
the door behind her. Shadows
bounced off the walls. I turned
to the table to my right where a card
from my 7th grade class lay.
We Miss You, in blue
and green letters.

Because of a birth defect
my esophagus kept closing.
I was unable to eat.
The dilatations weren't working—
I'd had hundreds, three
since Christmas—it was February.
The doctors told my mother
she should pray for a miracle.

Looking back, the miracle wasn't
the fact that I survived, but that I was spared,
like any sick kid is spared,
from responsibilities and expectations,
from a life in the factories
with men who wake
in the chill before dawn and labor
till after night falls, spared
from men who grow old and bitter,
never truly living the life they dreamed.

LETTER TO DAMIAN, FROM THE SPINNING WHEEL

Dear Damian, it's 2 a.m. here, under the blue neon. Snow
outside, guys in the back shooting darts and the jukebox
is playing *Skynyrd*, again. You should see this blonde in orange stripes—
what an ass. Not much else, really. Same old
same old. I told myself I'd stay in tonight—give
the liver a rest—but here I am. Lonely? Depressed? Sick
of my room, of reading Rilke? I confess to all. It sure is strange
though, the things you fixate on, sitting alone in a crowd,
like metabolism, or those plastic tubes on the ends of shoe laces,
other things, too, like time and how easy it is to keep everything
inside, to go through life never really knowing anyone
or eternity. How many people here do you suppose are thinking
about eternity? Fact is, sometimes I don't know whether I'm among the living
or the dead, but when I'm holding a beer, or whiskey, I feel
almost like, like Clint Eastwood. Anyway, enough about me.
I'm rambling. I just thought I'd write to say what's up? See how life
in the Great North Woods is treating you, the new job, the poems,
the wife and kids, to tell you how often I think of Elk Horn
and that summer we drove cross country, nights we sat atop
that old school bus of yours, in awe of the stars.
Your friend always.

MR. SANTO AND NAPOLEON

Mr. Santo used to teach tenth grade
History. He loved the Napoleonic wars
And horse racing, cried
over Mussolini and Bridgette Bardot.
I remember one Sunday
I saw him and his family at church
and after, at Davidson's Restaurant.
His wife looked like an Italian
starlet, but talked with a Cajun drawl.
Today I see Mr. Santo at the grocery store,
where I work part-time as a cashier.
He comes in every morning before ten,
for a twelve pack of beer.
His face is red and bloated
like road-kill. Sometimes he stands
in my line for hours, waiting
for the manager to leave,
knowing I won't charge him.
He tells me the same story,
of how his love for Napoleon,
Mussolini, Bridgette Bardot, even his wife
couldn't compare to his love
for the horses and booze.
He tells me how he lost his house
to the mob and his wife
to the cook at Davidson's.
I put his beer in a paper bag and wish
him good day. He says he doesn't go
to church anymore, but that each beer
is a bead on the rosary he stole
from St. Mary's and carries
like a good luck charm in his pocket.

Dream Of Return

I can't count the times I've dreamed of leaving,
of standing on a hill somewhere,
looking down on it all:
the muddy lake, empty store fronts
and sidewalks, the power plant
with its mountain of coal,
used car lots, parking lots,
factories, churches, diners, grocery stores
and for sale signs, all the faces
that pollute my memory with a feeling
of both belonging and not belonging,
the house I grew up in, its ceiling, forever
leaking. I remember how
my mother and I
would place pots, pans,
buckets and cups, all around
to catch the water that seemed to drip
for days after the rain stopped,
the sound of Elvis or some Christian
folk music blasting from an old turn table
and the sight of my mother at the stove,
checking our *Swanson* TV dinners:
cigarette burning between clenched lips,
her hair a swirl of violet,
or the yellow linoleum that shined
brighter than any sun,
somehow reflecting
all the quiet desperation that house could hold,
or that town, even,
that certain longing for something
people find hard to name:
a feeling or phrase, overheard
at a bar or on a talk show.
Hope, love, or God, maybe,
maybe, *Win For Life, One
Lump Sum,* or the simple pleasure
of watching humming birds at a feeder.

So many nights I'd lie awake
dreaming of all the places I'd go,

all those unknown cities, towns and countries
that filled my head like so many dates, facts
and phone numbers I've grow to forget.
I'd see myself standing by the railroad tracks
like Thomas Wolfe—
back pack and book in hand,
my hair mussed by the breeze, eyes
wide—waiting for a train
that no longer stopped
and now, now that I've left
I only dream of returning.

Nowhere

I'm doing nearly 80 on the curves,
wind in my eyes, west
on the lake road
past Canadaway Creek
where the first shots of the War of 1812
were fired, past the country club
and lumber yard.
I drive by *Sam's Fruit Company*, see
a group of migrant farm hands
dressed in cowboy shirts
and blue jeans, stand
around crates of cabbage,
smoking cigarettes, their faces like icons,
carved out of dark wood,
oriental and somber,
the kind you find at church lawn fairs
and thrift shops. Around the bend
a sea of grape fields, a tractor,
wildflowers and a white cross
to mark where two teenagers
flipped their car.
The sun is going down like a giant,
fiery peach and the moon
is almost transparent, hanging there
in the south east: a disembodied skull.

GOING HOME

Across from the Babe Ruth Field—
where Eddie Zappie pitched three perfect games
and could've made it,
if not for booze and Stacy Watson—
I kick the dust in the parking lot
at the old steel mill
where both my grandfathers did time,
watch the sun through broken
windows, the bricks and rust, ten years
since anyone worked here.

Downtown it's just as quiet,
a few old men on benches and kids
on bikes racing red lights.
All the stores went in '75,
now there's a Wal-Mart out by the Thruway.

On Center Street it's the same fat girl
behind the counter at the convenient store,
the same empty box cars
on the Third Street overpass and at Sara's Tavern,
the same faces drink the once local draft,
day after day, like the old women
who chant novenas and lust
after the priests at St. Mary's.

I can hardly imagine what Dunkirk was like
when my mother was young, let alone
in 1851, when the first train arrived with President Fillmore
and Daniel Webster onboard.

There are people here who talk of leaving,
but only go as far as *Bruce's Corner Store,*
or the Greek diner at the dock.
Maybe it's the view of the hills to the south,
or the three smoke stacks
of the electric plant at sunset, that keep us here,
or maybe it's the sound of my own voice,
reciting the streets named for birds and fish
as if they were the names of saints.